Sam –
   I hope this book inspires
you to define what you'd like
in life and helps you Get There!

                    Ken

GET THERE!

Chart Your Course to Financial
Abundance and Live the Life You Desire

By Ken Kladouris

ISBN-13: 978-1725988040

ISBN-10: 1725988046

Table of Contents

Dedication

To the inspired.

Acknowledgments

I would like to thank my family and friends for your support and encouragement.

To my coaches, mentors and teachers that have helped me along my journey, thank you.

To my clients, thank you for entrusting me and allowing me to be a part of your life and for sharing your stories with me; you add meaning to my work.

To the team who helped me with this book, Donna, Matt, Jamie, Lisa, Nancy, Jayme and Alexis, thank you. Working with each of you through this process has made the book so much more.

To Abella, thank you for your insight and guidance. You were the first person to read this book, which meant a lot to me.

I am grateful to each and every one of you, thank you!

Introduction

IT WAS A beautiful, sunny day in Southern California. A cool Pacific breeze filled the sails as I cruised down the coastline. The boat gently rocked with a flow that lulled me into a state of deep relaxation as the sunlight glinted off the waves. Toward the horizon a pod of dolphins splashed and played with each other, while overhead a flock of birds flew in a perfect V formation. It was an ideal moment. Everything seemed to have been placed there for my enjoyment. I couldn't help but think how lucky I was.

It was all the more special because it was so unlikely to happen. Less than a year before, I knew nothing about sailing. I'd never stepped foot on a sailboat and I couldn't imagine spending my days captaining a vessel down the coastline. I wouldn't have been able to picture a day like this, let alone experience it so fully.

So how did I get there? Twelve months before, I decided to give sailing a chance. I had always loved being on the water and I wanted to feed that passion. I was already familiar with power boating and I wanted to expand my horizons. I reasoned that I wouldn't be able to fully understand sailing by taking a single class so I set my sights higher. I made it my goal to acquire a basic sailing certification. That way I would have a chance to really see what it was all about. I'd learn the ins and outs of the activity, I'd learn the jargon, and I'd build up some muscle memory along the way. After I had made that pact with myself, I signed up for a course.

Lessons were difficult. The basic maneuvers were counterintuitive. I couldn't pick a destination and aim for it the way I did on a powerboat. I had to consider the wind and how it affected my craft. Execution of the ideas from the classroom hadn't translated on the water yet; my actions were still based on habits. I stayed the course and by the sixth lesson, things started to click. Finally, everything was going right.

Or so I thought.

Then one day as I was walking through the marina I noticed a new boat moored in the slips. The boat was gorgeous and immediately caught my eye. It was 40 feet with clean lines, a wide cockpit with teak accents, dual helms, and all the conveniences you could want down below. It was a big jump from the 20-foot harbor boats I was learning on. Without realizing it, I had begun to daydream about how great it would be to sail that boat off into the horizon. The fun my friends and family would have on short day cruises or long weekends to Catalina Island. Suddenly, my goal had evolved. I found out that the boat was owned by a local charter company which had its own certification program. I immediately signed up for their course and approached it with a new enthusiasm. I was all in. A certification was now just a means to an end, a way for me to achieve my enhanced goal of sailing that dream boat into the ocean and feeling all the freedom that came with it.

***

So, there I was on that idyllic Tuesday afternoon, feeling the breeze and getting rocked by the tide on the deck of a sailboat. I was enjoying my life to the fullest. I was living the life I wanted, enjoying the freedom I had planned for myself. I knew at that very same moment, countless others were sitting at the office or stuck in traffic on the highway. Really, I was no different from them and they were no different from me—I simply knew what I wanted and took steps to get there.

Why didn't everybody do this? Why couldn't they? It was in that moment I realized I needed to be more deliberate in helping individuals define and achieve their goals. I knew from my own experience that this worked. I could use my knowledge and passion for finance to help them draft plans and investment portfolios to keep them on track to achieving their goals. With a little help, I knew they could live out their passions and desires.

So many people go through life trying to achieve more, finish more, make more money. Instead, ask yourself what are the things you wish you were doing on a Tuesday afternoon? What are you passionate about? What is your purpose? This book is a tool to help you identify what you truly want and find the reasons why you want those things. It will provide you with the burning desire to achieve them, to take action, to create the path for you to Get There!

Ken Kladouris
Newport Beach, CA

.

CHAPTER 1

Master A Vision

Go confidently in the direction of your dreams.
Live the life you have imagined.

- Henry David Thoreau

"MY LIFE IS perfect," Michelle said to me. "My relationship with my family is the best it has ever been, my business is going strong, I have all of the clients I need, I have the income I want, plus I have the freedom to travel and spend time with my kids. I would have to give it a lot of thought to find if there is anything more I would want in my life."

How many of us can say that? I was happy for her, as just a few years prior she was working long hours, always on the road, grinding away for a large firm. Burnt out from all the demands, she had decided to quit her job and chase her passion of helping people while having the flexibility to spend more meaningful time with her family and friends. She was an inspiration. She had the presence to define what she wanted in life and the courage to go out and make it happen.

With the tools in this book I hope you too can find out what your ideal life looks like, what financial goals will provide that lifestyle, and ways to leverage your time and money to assist you in moving forward. I would like to have that conversation with you.

What Does This Have to Do with Financial Advice?

When I talk with people at cocktail parties and backyard barbecues, the inevitable question is asked: "What do you do?" Once people find out I'm a financial advisor, the questions about specific investments usually come up, as they want to share an experience they had or want to get my opinion about the hot new stock they heard about. Then, after a little dialogue, I hear their perspective about how financial planning is difficult, so I will ask in return, "What about the planning process is hard?"

That's easy for most to answer, as there are numerous reasons why people do not put together a financial plan: I don't have time to sit and plan! I don't have enough money! I already have a 401(k)! I'm uncomfortable with risk! The markets are against people like me! I don't trust others with my money!

Whew! To be sure, these can seem like good arguments. Yet, when I ask, "What are your financial goals?" the same people aren't as quick to answer. Most even look at me blankly for several moments before saying they've never thought about their goals or they throw out a generic number, like I want five million dollars. If I ask what that dollar amount does for them or the "why" behind the number, that same blank stare emerges.

Start by stating a simple goal about your future. How do you want it to be? How do you see yourself?

My intention is to break down financial planning to its bare minimum, which is to start by stating a simple goal about your future. How do you want it to be? How do you see yourself? What is the life you envision? Once that goal for your future is defined, it serves as the basis of all other financial decisions. Putting together a plan is a given as you want to achieve your goals and are willing to pour yourself into them.

Once you know where you want to be in the future, you can then make the incremental small steps to get there.

The process of figuring out your goals, dreams, and wants is the hardest part of this process. We will take the time to do some introspective thinking, find out what you're looking for, and find the resources to help you achieve those goals through proper planning and leverage. There is a vast world of resources, experts and investments that can create a path to where you want to go in a fashion much easier than you imagine. All it takes is the proper planning and knowing where you're going. With that in place everything else will fall into line and you will easily move toward your goals.

Start from Now

People who have put off financial planning or are afraid of their financial future may think to themselves, I don't know enough about the markets or money just isn't my thing or I am bad with numbers. Intellectually, they know that a stable financial future is vitally important, but the concept gets wrapped up in emotions and self-doubt until it becomes something they don't want to think about. Often, they wish money situations would just work themselves out on their own. People often don't consider that they have the power to change their financial circumstances and make a positive impact in all areas of their lives.

What happens then? They procrastinate. Day by day and year by year, they put off planning, always allowing their immediate financial demands to dominate their thoughts. This cycle drains energy and overwhelms emotions. When the idea of saving for retirement pops into their minds, it strikes a fearful nerve. They beat themselves up for not starting it earlier. They become too afraid to look earnestly at the future. They scare themselves into paralysis and breathe a sigh of relief when those thoughts fade away and they can focus on their present situation again. Or, maybe they put together the beginnings of a plan, but never finish it. After a while, they abandon it all together. Then, low and behold, retirement is suddenly just a few years away—or so they hope—and only now can they react to the facts.

That's not an ideal scenario. There's a lot of fear and worry involved. Instead, that time can be filled with happiness and the pride of accomplishment. Right now, is the best time to figure out your goals and how to achieve them. The golden years, which should be filled by living out dreams and enjoying meaningful endeavors, deserve more thought than last-minute panic.

> *So, change it. Take things a little at a time, set some smart goals, and take full advantage of the luxury of time to help you along the way.*

Find What Matters

I remember when Jordyn first walked into my office. She was a successful business owner, owned numerous properties and was a mother. She had recently expanded her business and was feeling the time constraints on her personal life. She shared a story that opened her eyes to what was most important to her. It was 6 a.m. and her daughter came racing into her room, excited and nervous that Jordyn was going to finally make it to her soccer game. They got ready and headed to the fields, a warm cup of coffee in Jordyn's hands. When they arrived at the field, her daughter jumped out of the car and ran to say hi to a friend. Jordyn recalled the smell of the grass covered in morning dew and how the dew trailed behind her daughter, looking like glitter as the sun reflected off of it. She was completely happy watching her daughter in that moment. She took a seat on the sidelines and watched as the game started. Her daughter was playing hard, giving it her all. In the middle of the fourth quarter, Jordyn's phone rang as one of her properties had a plumbing issue and the tenants needed her. She walked away from the field to take the call and coordinate the fix. Meanwhile, her daughter managed to break away and score the go ahead goal. Her daughter immediately turned, looking to the sidelines for her mom's recognition and shared wink, but Jordyn wasn't there.

It was after that moment, seeing the disappointment in her daughter's eyes, that Jordyn recognized she needed more balance in her life. She decided right then that she didn't want to have to walk away from the field again.

Now, Jordyn has her goals in order and knows exactly what she wants. In our meeting, she articulated how she wanted to have more time to spend with her family, while continuing to run and grow her business. She was looking for a way to leverage her time and investment properties. She had been acquiring properties with the goal of having the rental income cover her living expenses. She had a few headache properties that were draining her time and energy, so we were able to facilitate the sale of those properties and for her to enter a passive real estate investment through a tax deferred exchange. She still received monthly income and did not have to worry about the daily burdens of those properties, while removing the mortgage debt from her personal financials.

This example shows that it's vital to know what is important to you and what you want to focus on. Once you have defined your values, your priorities and understand the why behind what you want, the rest of the plan will fall into place.

Our goal is to build a personal vision for your financial life. By taking some simple steps and the time to reflect and be honest with yourself, you will find deeper goals. If you can do that, take action on your goals and focus on the things you can control, you can have the future you desire.

CHAPTER 2

Identify Your Goals and Plan for Your Ideal Life

Don't set sail on someone else's star.

- African Proverb

NOT EVERYONE WILL have the moment of realization that dawned on Jordyn, when she clearly and instantly saw what she wanted and why. For most people, lightning doesn't strike so easily. Luckily, there are ways to find out who you are at your core and your personal "why"—the deep-rooted cause that drives you forward.

To start, think deeply about yourself and who you are. What drives you? What do you want from life? What makes you feel happy, safe, loved? Your answers are important. They will form the basis of your personal vision statement, which will become the map of your future.

The vision statement is your compass, a North Star that points you in the direction of the right answers.

When you come across hard questions or forks in the road, you can refer back to your vision statement, which will show you the way.

> *What drives you? What do you want from life? What makes you feel happy, safe, loved? Your answers are important.*

Your vision statement should reflect all aspects of the life you want. It will provide you the ability to start planning for the future and to create the outcomes you want, all with an internal dialogue that will propel you forward. The ability to know your "why"—the reason you get out of bed each morning, the reason you transfer that money into a savings account and the reason you enjoy your life—that is the benefit of taking the time to draft your vision statement.

Now it's time to create that statement. It starts with a document. It can be a paper journal, a new note on your phone, or an email to yourself. The medium doesn't matter. What matters is that it's somewhere you can easily find and has enough space so you can continue to use it for later exercises.

Take a few minutes to craft your own vision statement. It should describe your ideal life, the core of your being and the manifestation of your true desires. Your vision statement is aspirational, hopeful and incredibly personal. It is what speaks to the deepest part of you and encompasses all of your hopes and dreams.

There's no right or wrong way to do this. You can write a paragraph; you can write a page. As long as you write your innermost "why" in your document, the length doesn't matter. Do it now.

After this exercise, you will come away with a far better recognition of yourself and what you value. From this starting point, it will be possible to take a deeper dive into what is necessary for you to be happy and how you can create that happiness. You will wake up each morning with a purpose, a desire to be better and reason to reach for your goals. And you will have a plan in place and a feeling of how great it is to have the things you desire. This is about you, your goals, wants, desires, and creating your path to achieving them.

How incredible does it feel to have a vision of your future and to know what you want? You are further along than many people in financial planning—and most aspects of life—simply by crafting that vision of your future. It is a significant step forward and that should be acknowledged as a major accomplishment.

It can be helpful to think about your future plans like a trip or journey that you're undertaking. Since there are two points when you are taking a trip—where you are going and where you start—it's necessary to examine both. You already know where you are going, thanks to your vision statement, so it's time to examine where you are right now. That means examining how you got here. The things you have loved, watched, heard, even dreamt affect your perception of the events that occur in your life. Therefore, you need to understand why you see or react to events the way you do. This will help you start to find your "why."

Understand the Present

Imagine standing on the beach and looking out over a vast ocean. Close your eyes for a second and put yourself in that scene. How does it make you feel— Small? Excited? Lonely? Inspired? When you picture that scene in your head, what exactly do you see, what kind of scene exists in your imagination? One person may picture a welcoming world ready to be explored, while another might see a deep source of inspiration, and another might be seized by thoughts of sharks, undertows and rogue waves crashing down. The same general scenario will always yield different feelings for different people. It's time to figure out what brings out the best feelings in you. By examining and investigating the things that have made you happy, you can find a template to help create more happy moments in the future.

Exercise 1: Begin to Find Your Center

Ask yourself, what do I want in life? What is important to me? What is my purpose? What makes me feel happy and fulfilled? Take as long as you need and come up with at least 20 different answers. Write them all down in your document. Now think about the person you want to become. Do your answers describe that person as well? If not, write some more. You can make two lists, if that helps. Write down everything that comes to mind. Allow yourself the freedom to let the ideas flow.

I remember one client who told me that, more than anything else, she enjoyed the freedom that extra time afforded her—meeting friends, seeing her children, taking trips, spontaneously making plans. She wanted to make sure that her retirement allowed her that privilege, as she hoped to have grandkids and wanted to ensure she'd have the time to enjoy them.

Exercise 2: Examine Value

A financial plan outlines what you want your future to look like and how you want to spend your time. Ideally, everyone wants to maximize the time they spend doing things that make them happy.

Whether it's time, beliefs, objects, achievements or money, everyone gets to define their own value in life. Pull out your document and make a list of the things that you treasure. Leave room between each item you name, so you can add notes later. Do it now.

Once you've finished that list, read it back. Then, write in the reasons why you value each treasure you've listed. These can be short or long. Take as much time as you need. Remember, this list is only for you. Be honest and write for yourself.

Understand the Past

It may seem odd to plan for your future by looking at the past, but a good financial plan should speak to you about what you want your future to look like, and how you want to spend your time going forward. You want that time to be spent doing things that make you happy, don't you? It is therefore important to understand what creates that emotion inside of you—and why.

Now think of a moment in your life where you felt the most freedom, when you felt the most alive. Think about what you were doing, how old you were, and how that feeling manifested itself. Look around that mental picture—what do you see, hear, smell, taste? Hold that moment in your mind for a moment. Picture who is with you—are they making you happy, adding to your experience? Immerse yourself completely in that moment. Embrace every part of it.

Now, come back to the present. Keep in mind how great just re-living that made you feel.

Exercise 3: Your Best Moment

Write down that moment you just re-experienced. Describe it in as much detail as you need to re-live those feelings. Include notes about who was there with you, what else was happening at that point in your life, and what about that moment made it so special. This will become an anchor.

Can you bring together some of those ingredients again? What's stopping you?

Think about how moments like that occur for you and what you have to do to bring more of them into existence. Look at the notes you just made. Can you bring together some of those ingredients again? What's stopping you?

Thoughts and memories are powerful tools. They guide our actions and become our best predictors of the future. They can comfort us in times of stress and reorient our focus toward what is most important. If you can master the ability to truly embrace your best moments as you live them, not only will they become even better, you'll find that they happen more often.

Exercise 4: Repeat and Examine

Repeat Exercise 3 for other moments of happiness in your life. Try to find some from a different time. Maybe a great holiday when you were a child. Or when you first learned something new about yourself. Take note of all the details in those moments and why they blended into such a perfect momentary tapestry. What was different about them?

It's useful to re-read your vision statement after you have written down these people, places and events that brought you such joy. Ask yourself if the vision you described is in line with these moments of your happiness.

You'll want to make sure that these images are consistent—that your vision of the future, who you will be, what you want more of in life and why you want that, can all coalesce together and create a path forward. If they are out of alignment, it will be challenging to segue smoothly into the future, as you will be pulled in other directions and get off course, draining your energy and focus.

The most seamless method toward attaining your vision is to marshal all your energy in the same direction. That's why it will be necessary to make sure that you create an environment where you are automatically focused and your life is in line with your vision.

Bring your thoughts back to today. You can only be in this moment. Where you are right now is where you must be. At this second, you are the sum of your entire past experience and you hold all of your potential for the future. You can make the future to be as bright as you can imagine. You can be thankful for your past and how it has shaped you. But you cannot escape the present.

Did you ever fail a test, lose a treasured possession, blurt out something inappropriate? What about winning a big game, nailing a presentation, finding a partner? Everything that has happened to you provides you strength to achieve your ideal future, as long as you can learn from your mistakes, accept your defeats, and grow from your experiences.

Through this assessment of life, everyone will find things they enjoy, things they are indifferent about, and things they dread. If it weren't for the valleys and peaks in life, we would have no depth, no stories of trial, and no battlegrounds. So, embrace them— the good and the bad. Remember them and be grateful for the opportunity you have, right now, to learn from them.

Understand Yourself

Take the time to ponder your life. What about your life today do you enjoy most? Do you wish you could do more or have more of something? When you think about these wishes, think about the "why" behind them. If you enjoy the time with your kids, what makes it special for you? Is it the feeling you have being near them, the pleasure you get out of watching their experiences, the thrill of caring for someone you love? If you like that you have a place to live, what about it do you like? Is it the furniture and appliances you've acquired, the feeling of safety and comfort it provides, the friends, family and moments you get to share in that home?

A good plan accounts for all parts of life—not just the good times. You must know both sides of yourself to fully flourish going forward. When you understand how you react to both positive and negative situations, and why some experiences feel better than others, you'll be on your way to unlocking the deeper feelings that drive you. You'll be closer to knowing your true center and finding your "why."

Exercise 5: Examine the Other Side

What occurred recently that upset you? Can you remember? What was it about that moment that got under your skin and why did it have such an effect on you? Perhaps you offhandedly said something wrong at a party. Maybe you embarrassed yourself in front of your boss or an important client. Maybe your partner snapped at you over something trivial or your child took you for granted. Whatever it was, remember what you felt like in that moment. Did all your feelings stem from that event, or did it trigger something deeper inside of you? Were you already having an off day, in a rush, or do you always react that way when people do that or behave in such a manner? Take a deep breath, and make a list of those things that detract from your happiness.

Now go back and read over both the positive and negative lists you have created. Do you notice any themes? Do any insights emerge? Do you notice patterns? Do your worst feelings come from disappointing your friends and family? When you let go of your principles? Or maybe when you didn't speak up or take action, even though you know you should have? Planning for your best life also means limiting what will hurt you along the way.

> *Money is not your goal. It is only a means to achieve your goal.*

As you look at those moments, how many instances explicitly deal with money? Some might, but not the ones that really hurt. Money does not usually conjure the overwhelming emotions that true experience can. It may add to your ability to experience great moments, but it is not where passion resides. Money is only a tool, and like any tool it can be used to help you along. It is said that it's a poor workman who blames his tools. Money is not happiness. It probably didn't figure into your life's best moments. Keep that in mind. Money is not your goal. It is only a means to achieve your goal.

If you need to mend relationships, treat yourself better, follow your dreams more or simply enjoy the everyday moments that pass you by, keep that in mind as you plan for your financial future.

CHAPTER 3

Embark on Your Path

The best time to plant a tree was 20 years ago.
The second best time is now.

- Chinese Proverb

WITH YOUR VISION statement of who you want to be, a better-defined purpose in life, and a clear understanding of who you are and why you are that way, you have all the necessary elements to start plotting a path forward. Your destination—the life you want—won't just happen. It is only possible if you take the time to figure out what it is, what it looks like, and how you will feel once you've achieved it. Think of it like a New York City airport. If you've been there a few times, it's a breeze. You understand the layout of the terminals, know where baggage claim is and can navigate the parking areas with ease. But if it's your first time, the experience is decidedly different. You have no idea where you are going, the crowds can feel overwhelming and you are hurrying through, looking for signs to help tell you where to go.

Wouldn't it be better to react in the right manner and move fluidly toward your goals?

This is a very similar example to your goals. If you have seen yourself living your goals and achieving them, when you get there and the opportunity arises, you will know what to do. You won't be lost and looking for help. Wouldn't it be better to react in the right manner and move fluidly toward your goals?

In the previous chapter, you looked into your daily life and found out which activities you like, which ones you wanted to be able to have more of, and which things you simply do without much thought or care. Now, as you explore the future and investigate your desires, it is important that you allow yourself to dream. You need to go beyond the limits you currently see in front of you because they may be holding you back. This may require you to re-examine how you think about yourself and your future. Only if your goals are in line with your vision statement and the things that bring more happiness into your life, will you effortlessly move closer to them. If you want to be happy and you have a plan that leads you toward increased happiness, you should naturally move toward it.

Time and Goals

Have you ever noticed how some people always have time to do fun stuff, no matter how busy they are? Every Saturday they are on their bicycles, pedaling down the street like they don't have a care in the world. They are constantly posting pictures of fishing trips. It feels like they're on vacation every other week! Do they possess some secret or perhaps have a superhuman ability to get work done? Maybe. But probably not.

> *What many people don't realize is that if you want to harness your passion, you have to put some of that energy toward your finances.*

People may wonder to themselves, "If these folks are truly that busy, how is it possible that they have time to do all of these things or the money to afford it?" They find ways because they are passionate about doing so. These folks know how to make the most of small opportunities here and there to squeeze out extra time or money. Whether their passion is yoga, hiking, technology, fashion, cars or boats, their embracement of it drives them toward high achievement. Their passion pushes them to go that extra mile. Everyone can access that same kind of passion if they know what drives them.

For me, it's the water. I have a passion to be on the water and I will find the time and money to make sure I can experience it. It doesn't matter whether it's racing around on a powerboat or taking a relaxing cruise on a sailboat, I'm in. What many people don't realize is that if you want to harness your passion, you have to put some of that energy toward your finances.

Everyone has a passion, just like everyone has a dream. Sometimes those dreams stay a secret because the dreamers are afraid someone will tell them their dream is not realistic. Sometimes people are too embarrassed by their dreams to share them.

When that happens, those dreams feel so far removed that the dreamer cannot see the possibility of achieving them. The dreams shrivel up and waste away. Other times, dreams are proudly spoken about. They are always present in the dreamers' lives and their repetition animates them into life.

Whether your dream is to have an emergency fund, to buy a new car, to travel, to buy a new house or to start a business—whatever it may be—you owe it to yourself to speak your dreams into existence and to try and reach for them.

Exercise 6: Start to Think About Your Goals

Consider the questions, "What do I really want? What are my big goals?" Get out your document and write down both of those questions and your answers. Then continue to write out your thoughts for a few minutes. Invest a little time with this; it's important. Remember that your goals can apply to anything—health, relationships, money, etc. Let your imagination flourish. When you picture this future, ask yourself where you are, who are you with, what do you do? Make a list of at least five things you want. Writing down your goals is invaluable to success in all aspects of life. This brings you one step closer to achieving them.

Once the list is finished, go back and re-read the list you created in Chapter 2, when you outlined the things, people and qualities in your life that increased your happiness. Do you notice any overlap there? Do you get a sense that as you attain these goals, you will be happier? If not, revisit Exercise 6 again. You want your happiness and your goals to intermingle. Otherwise, you may be planning for a life that doesn't bring you joy.

The list you just created is a crucial step. Living your goals first in your mind makes it much more likely that they will come to fruition. Visualization like this is a powerful tool. But it works both ways. Don't let yourself think about all the reasons you can't achieve the goals or why they're not possible. Try to focus only on the positive emotions that occur as you think of them.

From Dream to Reality

The next step is to examine the real motivations that lie behind these goals. Often, there are internal needs hidden deep within us that manifest as physical desires. A longing for a sports car, for example, might really be a need to feel powerful and in control. A desire for a big home may mask a want for a family to fill it. Keep this in mind as you continue to think about your goals. Be sure to examine the motivations behind what you want.

The "why" to all of your future goals is vitally important. That "why" will give you the strength, the energy, the dedication and gusto to strive forward, to wake up each morning feeling in control of your financial future, energized to overcome any challenge that may try and stand in your way. The confidence that radiates from embracing your vision statement will make any obstacle pale in comparison.

Your goal will become too important to let something derail you. Those inconveniences that used to cause an immediate reaction in you, maybe even frustrate you, will no longer garner your attention. The momentum you are creating forward, toward your goals, will simply run over those bumps in the road.

The "why" is what makes you take real action and inspires you to be more, to leave laziness and excuses in the rearview mirror, and to strive forward.

Figuring out the motivation behind your goals is so powerful that it will give you the energy to make it real. It is the well of resolve that you can draw from to achieve anything. Your motivation lies deeper than surface-level thoughts, you'll need to get a few layers below the surface to access it, like peeling an onion back. But the results are worth it.

The "why" is what makes you take real action and inspires you to be more, to leave laziness and excuses in the rearview mirror, and to strive forward.

Exercise 7: Find the "Why"

Now I'd like you to pick one of the goals from the list you made in Exercise 6 and write it down on the top of a piece of paper. You will be taking a deep dive into this goal and finding your "why." You need to figure out what about this goal is so powerful that it will make you take real action to achieve it; you need to know why you will take a little extra time or energy each day to move closer to it. You will have to go deeper than surface-level thoughts, like breaking open a pistachio shell to get to the good part. You want to create a list of as many reasons as possible to why you want to have that goal. You can have as many reasons as you like but there should be at least ten reasons why you want to achieve the goal.

Once you've finished, clear your head and look back over the list with a fresh mindset. Ask yourself why you want these things. Create a second list of those reasons. It may take a little more time and thought to come up with, so allow yourself space to answer it thoroughly. Once you're happy with that, repeat this process again. Do it as many times as necessary until you have a few core reasons, a top three, as to why you want to reach a specific goal.

What comes to your mind as you wrote those down? How does your list look? Is it longer than you expected? Are the reasons as meaningful to you as you hoped they would be? As you read your reasons does a passion start to burn in your mind and soul to achieve your goals? Can you feel yourself being pulled toward it? Your passion should start to spark and your soul should begin to seek new ways to achieve your goals. If this isn't happening, you have the wrong goals or the wrong why. Go back over this chapter and revise your answers until they feel good to you. Remember, this is about planning for your ideal life. If you want to build a financial plan that allows you to live out your dreams, those dreams need to be well defined and understood. Completing this portion of the plan to the fullest will help you later.

You now have an extensive list of what you want in your future and why. Now ask yourself, what is it worth to have these dreams and goals in my future? What would I be willing to forgo today in order to have those things later? I'm not a saying to forget everything or deprive yourself of all happiness. Quite the opposite! Focus on things that bring you joy today and start limiting those that you despise. The things that drain you financially and/or emotionally, or that are distracting or limiting, have a major effect on your life. Those limiting beliefs lessen your ability to move swiftly toward your goals. The value you place on your future, the eagerness you have to get to that ideal place in life, will make you that much more willing to reach your goals and strive forward each day.

I recall working with a client, Jill, whose chief goal was to retire near her family. She worked in California but wanted to move back to Tennessee, where all her family lived. Yearning for a good job and nice weather, she'd left for the West Coast twenty years earlier, and now found herself almost a continent away from her children, grandchildren, nieces and nephews. Jill's goal was to be a bigger part of their lives and that meant leaving California. Thanks to a clear goal, we were able to put together a step-by-step plan to get her back to Tennessee with enough money to retire. She was already close to retirement and had been saving during her careers, so we made some minor changes to her portfolio. Jill utilized different investments, sold her investment property in California, and purchased a different investment that allowed her to maintain exposure to real estate, defer her taxes, and receive monthly checks all while leaving the management and headaches behind. These investments combined to provide the cash flow Jill needed to live comfortably in Tennessee.

It was a combination of Jill's deep desire to reunite with her family and the investment opportunities available to her that allowed her to move sooner than expected, with more financial means than she thought she would have. If Jill could do it, so can you. She is no different than you. Her story is not unique. You should be energized and know that it is possible for you as well.

CHAPTER 4

Define Your Goal

For tomorrow belongs to the people who
prepare for it today.

- African Proverb

HOW GREAT DOES it feel to have a vision of the
future? You have a huge picture of your dreams and
your passion is attracting you to it. Now it is time to
create a plan to attain your goals.

What you want comes to fruition with intention and
purpose. Energy and thought, combined with
decisive action, can do incredible things to change
your life— more than you can do alone. Why?
Because direction solves problems. You can try and
try to move forward, but if you don't know where
you're going, you might be spinning in circles,
exhausted from all the work. Without direction, you
expel all the energy, waste all that time, yet no
further progress is made, and you find yourself
sitting in the same exact place, feeling defeated. Why
is that? What can you do differently?

It is time to be deliberate with your energy and intention. You can also think of your savings, your money, as a kind of energy.

Unless you know where your destination is, any decision you make—whether to turn here or there—will feel right, since no choice can be wrong. This can make you feel like you are doing all the right things, even when you haven't been. The goal is to know where you are headed, and to use that knowledge to make those small, correct decisions that move you closer to your goals. It is time to be deliberate with your energy and intention.

Your Fuel

Realize that your energy is an important tool on your journey toward your vision. Energy is what gets you from where you are now to where you want to be.

You can also think of your savings, your money, as a kind of energy. For example, you can choose to forget about your money and let it sit lazily by doing nothing. In that case, your money is wasting its energy, sitting in an account earning no return, while you work hard to earn more money to put into that account to do nothing. Or, on the other hand, you could be deliberate with how you use your savings and allow your money to use its energy to work for you.

Your money can start to create a return that adds more savings to your account, giving you more money to pursue further opportunities. That is how you can harness the energy of money, to align with your goals and achieve them quicker.

Your MAPS

When starting to think about your goals, it is important that they are specific and measurable to you. To assist you with your goal setting, I have created a simple technique to help you draft your goals. It is as easy as creating MAPS to your goals. Your goal should be:

M - Measurable
A - Actionable
P - Personal
S - Specific

Measurable. Your goals need to have some type of measurability or standard, so that you know how you are progressing, if changes need to be made, and, of course, when you have achieved it. Instead of creating a vague goal like "Pay down debt," think about putting your goal into terms that you can define and see. A better goal would be "Pay off my $8,000 in debt by next year." This way, you can measure your progress. With a definitive measure, you will have the ability to track yourself through time, and be able to develop a sense of accomplishment along the way, which will not only make you feel great, but also keep that fire burning inside of you to achieve your goal and strive forward.

Actionable. The goal needs to be actionable. What that means is that you need to be able to have an impact on your outcome by actively doing something. If your goal is not actionable, then it is merely a dream and you should want better than that for yourself. You want to be able to take the reins and use your energy to attain your goals. So, as you think of your goal, what are the steps— the actions— that you can take to move yourself forward? Small steps have a big impact, so think of all the activities you could be doing that will help you reach that goal. For example, a goal like "I made a full contribution to my IRA this year" has several actionable steps that you can take to get there. Maybe you need to open an IRA, set up an automatic contribution, or send in a check. All of these steps empower you to take action toward the goal.

Personal. These goals need to be personal. You have to feel yourself living your final outcome and you have to want to get there. If a goal "sounds good" but doesn't resonate with you, it will be hard to make yourself stick to your plan in the future. A goal of "Buying a vacation house in Del Mar to bring my family together more often" is a perfect example of creating a goal that is tailored to one person's specific wants and desires. No outside party can make you want something, so make sure that you have been true to yourself and that you truly want the outcome you've chosen.

Specific. Goals that are too general produce the general result: failure. This is why so many New Year's resolutions don't last. "Lose some weight" sounds like a fine goal, but it's too abstract to apply directly to any one person. The list of specifics you made earlier will help you customize your goal to suit your particular situation. Instead of simply "doing better with money," your goal should include how and why you want to make a change. Do you want to save for a rainy-day fund, put away money for your children's college education or maybe buy a new car?

The more specific your goal is, the more real it will be to you and the easier it will be for you to accomplish it. If you take these small steps toward crafting your goals, a sense of meaning and ownership of the goal will fill your spirit and you will start to move confidently in the direction of your dreams. The financial success you imagine is around the corner and you are heading in that direction.

I was speaking with a client, Danielle, and the topic of goals came up. She lived a comfortable life, but had a feeling that she would act more freely and confidently if she had an extra $50,000 in a savings account. This was an achievable goal for her, but she had yet to achieve it. I asked her, "Danielle, have you written down your goal?" to which she responded affirmatively. Then I asked, "What actions have you taken to move toward your goal?"

And there was the block. Danielle had not spent any time doing the actions necessary to achieve the goal.

She decided that the next day she was going to go to the bank and open the savings account and deposit $100. Now $100 into an account in which you want to save $50,000 may not seem like a large amount, but it got the momentum started. She was now looking at an account, ready to go, ready to hold the $50,000 she wanted in it. Every day she looked at the account balance and, wanting to achieve her goal, she took every opportunity she could find to drop a few dollars in, creating even more momentum toward her goal. She found new ways to save money and was enjoying herself more than before.

Can you imagine that, saving more money and being happier? How wonderful would that be? As time passed, she continued to save, and after 18 months, she had it. Danielle achieved her goal and had the $50,000 in a savings account. It took less time than she expected, she had fun doing it and she has a new habit of saving. She also developed a higher sense of accomplishment and the security she was hoping for with the extra cushion of cash available if needed. She accomplished all of this while living how she wanted and having fun the entire time.

If she can do it, so can you. There is little difference between you. The amounts may fluctuate depending on your current situation, but with the motivation to achieve them and the small steps you will take, you will reach your goal.

Create Your Timeline

As Duke Ellington once said, "I don't need time. I need a deadline." Keeping with that premise, it is a good idea to break up your goals into four different time periods. A specific, short-term goal of $1 million in the bank is probably not going to help you if you have $500 in the bank. If your mind can't see it happening and you're not passionate about it, you will likely not put the proper energy into reaching that goal. If your goal is to grow your account from $500 to $1,000, that is something you can get behind. You will have more of an emotional tie to that goal, you can outline a path to get there and you will put in the effort to reach that goal. The success you imagine is just outside your grasp and you are heading toward it by getting this far. Be proud!

Exercise 8: One-Year Goals

The first time period contains things you would like to achieve within the year. A lot of people set goals each new year to start saving more, to create a budget or to become more financially responsible, all of which are great ideas! Yet very few people actually take the time to plan how they will accomplish those goals. You have already started with the intention of achieving more by doing these exercises. Start this one by thinking of the things that you say you're going to do each year and never achieve for whatever reason. Write those down. And write them down as if you have already achieved them. For example, instead of writing, I will save 5% of my income, write I saved 5% of my income. As another example, change I will have investment property to I own investment property. Or a final example: change I will find ways to create passive income to I have the passive income I desire.

Writing your goals in the past tense helps you because when you read those words, or hear them, you are telling yourself that your goals have been achieved, that you have already made it happen. With that you will begin to act and behave as though you have achieved your goals and you will slowly become the person who can accomplish those goals. When you are the person that has those things, you will find more opportunities to achieve your goals, and they will occur. Each year you say you're going to get these done, and this year you will.

Five-Year Goals

The next time frame to reach your goals is one to five years, and these goals are a little further out of reach. Remember earlier, the example of Danielle with her $50,000 in savings. Maybe her five-year goal is to save up $200,000. With smart savings and investing, that is reasonable. These goals might not have an emotional connection as strong as the year one goals, as they are a little further removed from you today, but as you feel yourself moving closer toward reaching your goals, you'll find that your energy will grow. Once you start down the path of success, you will enjoy the way it makes you feel.

You will realize more is possible and continue to reach further. When $50,000 becomes $75,000 and then $100,000, you'll start to believe even more that you can achieve your goals. That is why having the goal in mind is more important than knowing the entire process of reaching that goal. As you continue to move forward along the path to your goals, you will come to intersections and have to make choices on how to proceed. The route you take will be your own, and as you develop the ability to identify and act on opportunities, you will build the knowledge from previous successes and failures that will help guide you. During the process, you'll find you will have more energy to pursue even bigger goals. It's important not to let that newfound energy go to waste.

One great way to capitalize on your new skills and abilities is to partner with a professional financial advisor. A professional can help you make the most of your abilities and keep you alerted to new possibilities for growth. They can make sure you stay on track and keep you accountable. Most importantly, they can offer insights and connections. I love hearing stories of clients' successes and want to help in any way I can.

Exercise 9: Five Years Out

From job interviews to friendly conversations we have all heard the question, "So where do you see yourself in five years?" When you were asked this question you may have had a different answer based on the person asking or the situation surrounding the question and tailored your answer to meet the ideas of what they wanted to hear. But what you write down here is for you, no one else, and no one will tell you that you cannot do it or put you down for thinking so boldly. Be gentle on yourself and be truthful. It is imperative that you believe you can achieve them and want them for yourself. Other people can't give you the emotional energy to achieve your goals. Other people can't make you get out of bed each morning with a sense of purpose, with a "can do" attitude, full of excitement and life. You are the only one that has that control. All of your goals are going to require you to do certain things, so you will need to be prepared to do them. Going from $50,000 to $200,000, for example, doesn't happen without effort. The sum builds day by day, deposit by deposit. Change, even small change, can take time, energy, persistence and patience, all of which you will need to be willing to put into reaching your goals. So, listen to yourself and be wholehearted and pure in your reflection and ideas.

Five to Ten

In the next two time periods, you get to do a bit of fantasy thinking or bigger dreaming. In the last chapter, you envisioned your ideal life and the life events that you want to have.

You saw yourself living your dream and how amazing is that dream life. Can you see it again now? Can you feel that burn to get there, building momentum inside of you?

So now, think in the 5- to 10-year range. In 10 years, a lot can change or a lot can stay the same, depending on your desires. You clearly want to grow, develop and attain goals. So it is your intention to move forward over the next 10 years, right? In 5- to 10-years, what would you like to see, what is around you, where do you live?

Exercise 10: A Decade in the Making

Pull up that picture of your ideal life and future that you envisioned in the earlier chapters. Take that photo, that fine-tuned image of your future, and break it into two groups of goals.

The first group will be the 5- to 10-year attainable goals and the second is your 10 year goals. For the 5- to 10-year goals, you should feel that if all goes to intention, they will be attained, even if you do not see the path. Seeing the path or knowing all the steps is not important, those will come to you along the journey.

New inspiration or great ideas will spontaneously come to you and provide you with the right action or path to take. The main purpose here is to let yourself know where you want to be and who you want to be.

10 Years and Beyond

For goals of more than 10 years out, things are a little further removed. You can see them in your mind, but the path is even blurrier. That is fine. It is important to have thoughts larger than life, out of your grasp, to keep you ever expanding.

Remember, as you reach your one-year targets and carry the momentum forward to your future, you'll move closer to these 10-year goals and they will start to come into focus. You can see the building blocks, watch the events unfold in your life and know in your mind that these goals are yours.

Exercise 11: Life in the Future

Writing out these goals may feel like inventing a fantasy world. Get comfortable with that. As you come back to these goals over time, the fantastic elements will harden into more concrete images and you can begin to refine that vision. Write down a few 10-year plus goals right now, and indulge your inner dreamer. There are no wrong answers or goals, only people who are too afraid to try and reach for them.

For each goal, make sure you have a way to acknowledge that you achieved it. And once you get there, take a moment to cherish that experience, acknowledge that you reached the goal, take in that feeling of success and build on it. Take that energy and use it to push forward on to the next goal. You know you can do it.

How will you feel when you achieve your goal? You already know! See, you already hold all of the tools, skills and emotions for your success within you. You are the person, right now, in this moment, who has achieved all of these things. You don't need to wait for the material aspects to arrive; they will come in time. If something knocks you down or makes you feel unworthy, pick yourself up, let the feeling go and start over. Each new moment is new opportunity for you to create greatness.

Remember the feeling you felt earlier in this book, when you saw your future? You can pull those feelings up, to harness and feel them again, at any time. So, embrace all the things you will feel at that moment of achievement and take it in.

Now, how are you different from that success? Do you walk a little taller, hold your head up with a little more pride, and feel more confident in yourself? Feel all the things that you will feel at that moment and realize that you are that same person, and that you're feeling all of those feelings right now. Harness those emotions, embrace them, and use them to carry yourself forward into the future.

You will have success and added momentum toward your next goal. Each time you achieve a goal you will feel even better and build a deeper reserve of emotions to pull from, to move you toward your next achievement. Your added enthusiasm and self-belief continue pulling you closer and closer toward your goals.

The Day-to-Day

Great, now you have a timeline of your goals from short-term to long-term that can help guide you through your daily decisions. You can ask yourself at any point in time, are my decisions and actions moving me closer or further away from my goals? It'll be as simple as that. Is what I'm doing adding to my goal, is it moving me closer? Am I putting myself in a position to better my life and move toward my desires? These are the questions you will start asking yourself and eventually it will become habitual for you to automatically move toward your goals.

> *When you focus, you will begin to notice more opportunities. By focusing on the positive, more positives will come to be.*

When you are thinking about your financial goals, focus on the positives. Many times, it is easier to see the problems, the reasons why something won't happen. This causes you to lose the energy to push forward, which can lead to more negative thoughts, and then problems occur. That keeps you from reaching your goals. So rather than the negative, focus on the reasons it can happen. Focus on the sliver of light that's visible now. Where you place your attention is where more things occur. When you focus, you will begin to notice more opportunities. By focusing on the positive, more positives will come to be.

To help with this idea, think about buying a new car.

You go to the dealership and stroll around the showroom when, all of the sudden, a new white Range Rover catches your eye. You're drawn to its clean lines, solid frame and luxurious interior. Its paint glints in the sun. As an added benefit, you don't think you have ever seen one driving down the street before. You make the purchase. Ecstatic, you drive off the lot and immediately pull up next to the same Range Rover at the first light. Huh, you think. It could be a coincidence. You are right by the dealership after all. Then, on the drive home, you see another, then another. For weeks, not a day goes by that you don't see someone else driving your new car down the road. What gives? Did everyone go out and buy a new Range Rover? Are more of them on the road this week than last week? Probably not. It is more likely that since that specific Range Rover drew your attention and awareness, you are now noticing them everywhere. Using this same principle, if you keep your attention on your goals and why you can have them, you will notice more opportunities in everyday life to move toward your goals. Focus on your goals and watch them appear.

CHAPTER 5

Accomplish Your Goals, One Day at a Time

A journey of a thousand miles
begins with a single step.

- Chinese Proverb

ALL OF YOUR goals, from where you want to be in 30 days or 30 years, start with daily habits. The actions you perform every day help define the person you are and determine where you are going. You have already determined where you are today and created a personal vision statement for your life. From there, you outlined your short-term goals and long-term goals. Those short- term goals are just outside your reach, where you need to stretch just a little bit to achieve them. With those small wins, momentum is built toward the medium- and long-term goals. So how can you set yourself in motion, how can you become an unstoppable driving force toward your goals?

Let's start by looking at your daily habits. It is easy to feel that you are always in control, always aware of what you're doing and why you're doing it. There is this sense that you consciously think and analyze everything that you do. I know I felt that way, too! Then one day I was talking to a client, Lucas, about a trip he had just taken and how he had spent substantially more than he anticipated. He recalled everything he bought and explained how he felt each item was necessary. It wasn't until all of those purchases showed up on a monthly bill that he looked back, thinking maybe he had gotten wrapped up in the emotion and excitement of the trip and bought more than he needed. Lucas was late to the game—he only had the charges on the credit card statement to remind him of how much he had spent. And now that the money was spent, Lucas was justifying to himself and others why he needed those things.

Now, many of us have some thought process and try to take a pause before making large purchases. Usually you don't run out every day and buy large appliances, cars or extravagant trips. But on occasion, there is that day you need one, so you shop around a little bit, look for the best price and return home with it. Most other days, you go about your routine, doing the ordinary activities without much thought or consideration for what you are doing. It comes naturally and seems to flow from one activity to the next. You take the same route to the office, have the same coffee, and have the same favorite lunch place. It all seems to play out just as it is supposed to.

Having a goal fall into your lap, when you didn't do anything or any amount of work to achieve it, is highly unlikely.

With minor work and a little more consciousness of action, these little tweaks of habits, done without even thinking, can lead to achieving your goals without the tremendous work of doing it all at once. Having a goal fall into your lap, when you didn't do anything or any amount of work to achieve it, is highly unlikely. Rather, people who get what they want do so because they take the time to acknowledge their desires, draft plans to get them, and take real action to move forward.

Take It One Month at a Time

Taking the time to review your monthly spending activity is an important aspect of your financial future. That knowledge, that information about your life is very valuable.

Exercise 12: Analyze Spending Habits

Print out your monthly bank statements and credit card statements so you can review them. As you go through the statement cross out the necessities, the things you need to live your daily life. With those crossed out, find the smallest amount that you spent over the past month. What is it? How frequently did you make that purchase? Are there purchases you can barely remember? Did you think, oh yeah, we went out for lunch that day and I spent $100 for no reason or I got dragged out by people whose company I don't even enjoy and spent $50 to have a dreadful time? These are the actions, the steps that you can eliminate and make an impact on your future. Does it feel like every time you go out, even if for no reason, somehow you still spend $100 or more?

In what areas can you make small changes that will better your life?

There are so many people I know that have that exact same feeling. If they could only change their habits and not go out as often, and instead do something they enjoy more, they could put that $100 they would have spent into a savings account and watch it grow. Those small changes can bring more happiness, more money and more drive to keep making other small changes to improve their lives. In what areas can you make small changes that will better your life?

Now, it's important not to think that you can just eliminate certain behaviors and instantly change your life. Rather, you should try to supplement an unenjoyable activity or action with another that you enjoy, maybe even more. When the trigger happens, the call from the neighbor you don't even enjoy who's always dragging you out, maybe you'll say you are busy tonight and allow yourself to do whatever it is that makes you happy instead. The freedom to go for a walk, read, do anything that has a positive impact on you emotionally. After a few times of refocusing your energy, when the trigger is presented your new action will become more and more natural. You will start to automatically make a lunch in the morning or make a coffee instead of grabbing one on the way to work. These minor changes will become habits that can make a drastic impact on your life in the future by building up slowly over time.

Now you might think this is all fine and dandy, but you want to enjoy your life and experience things, and you should! There's an easy way to do this. Think about your short-term goals. Picture them in your mind, feel what it's like to have those things, to have accomplished those things. As you picture yourself achieving and living out those goals, you will be enjoying your life in the moment as you strive toward the life you want. You'll be deliberate in your actions and start to live the life you feel is better for you. The clarity that will come as the fog of daily life dissipates will be empowering. You will go from feeling a lack of control or focus with no clear destination to an overwhelming feeling of joy and happiness in your life. You will be living a life with intention, behaving and holding yourself out as the person you want to be, and will create the desire and outcomes you want. Can you feel that excitement? Can you feel how much power you have in your life? Take that power and use it, create the things you want, be happy, be you. Go out and get there!

Hold Yourself Accountable, The Easy Way

Let's take a small amount of time and look at where you can make minor changes in daily life to affect the best change in your future. Today, shake it up a little bit by taking some time to think about your spending habits before you spend any money. I know a lot of people look at their monthly statements and make sure everything balances and is accounted for. If you are anything like me, you might go to Starbucks almost unconsciously, never realizing how much money you're spending on coffee. So, although reviewing monthly activity is a great habit, it is not what you want to do here, which is to review the purchase before you make it.

Exercise 13: Your Spending Journal

One of the best ways I've found to accomplish this is to keep a spending journal. When you take the time to grab a journal and write down what you are going to spend money on before you buy it, you short circuit your brain's autopilot and think deliberately about what you are doing. While you are reaching for that journal or pulling out your phone to note the purchase, think about if you need to make the purchase to move closer to your goals and wants or if you are simply buying it because that's what you have always done. I like to write down the item and cost before I do anything, then if I decide to forgo the purchase, I circle the amount; if I make the purchase, I leave the entry alone. This gives you the opportunity to consciously think about the purchase and if you really need it. If it is something that you need or moves you toward your goal, you will move forward with the purchase and feel good about it. If it is not needed or helping with your goals, if it is something you only do because you're bored, you may choose not to spend the money.

Work with your spending journal for 30 days so that you have different routines and environments to experience the benefits of journaling and shed light on your spending habits. After the 30 days is up, take out your journal and review it. Observe the length of the journal, how many times you thought about spending money and count how many circles you have. Are there more circles at the end of the month or the beginning? Add up the amounts within your circles to see how much you saved with this easy exercise. You will be pleasantly surprised by your results.

Put that extra savings to work toward your goals and witness how much faster and effortlessly you get there.

The power of the knowledge you will have gained from that experience can be dramatic. You may find new things you enjoy, things you no longer want to spend money on, areas where you want to make changes, and the ability to save more money. Put that extra savings to work toward your goals and witness how much faster and effortlessly you get there.

Take Small Steps

I can understand if you are still questioning how these small, seemingly inconsequential changes can lead to major accomplishments. When something looks hard, it may be difficult to muster up the energy and desire to take action. With everything going on in your life, the idea of adding one more big task is overwhelming. A feeling of I can't do that may set in so that you don't take on the challenge. Your mind can convince you that adding one more thing is something you don't need to do or want to do, and will create the excuses you need to feel comfortable not taking action. But taking action is often a lot easier than you think.

Let me illustrate what I mean. I had a list of books that were recommended to me by various individuals over the years, but I had never gotten around to reading any of them because I was too busy. Then one day I decided to download the electronic versions so I could read them whenever it was convenient and I had a couple minutes to spare. Whether at home, the office, a waiting room at the doctor's, or anywhere else I might be, I would pull up the book and chip away at a few pages. Soon, I was finished with the first book, then the second, and all of a sudden, I had time every day to read. I never really looked at the page counts or had any reference to the size and thickness of the book in physical form. Then one day I was out on a three-day sailing trip with a group of six people. We had just anchored for the night and everyone was getting settled and unwinding from the long day. As I started the barbeque I noticed one of the guys walking to the bow of the boat with what I would call a massive book—it was thicker than most textbooks. I looked at him in awe, thinking how much dedication that would take to get through and how nice it would be to one day sit and find pleasure in reading a book like that. As we were getting ready to eat, he walked back from the bow and I noticed the cover of the book and started laughing. I had read that book months ago! I was shocked. Since I had never had the opportunity to see the hurdles, the challenge of its massive size, my mind didn't have an opportunity to psyche me out or put up excuses as to why I couldn't do it. I just started reading. I took the small steps, here and there, on a daily basis and got through it.

In the same fashion, you can take seemingly little steps, which likely will seem inconsequential to you at the time and won't give you a sense of great accomplishment. Yet as you add up those actions, you will look back at your huge accomplishment. All without the strain and pressure of thinking you needed to do it all at once.

Many times, you may think about the hard work, time and energy you put into trying to reach a goal and feel that you have not gotten very far, that all of your effort has done little to further you. Yet these small, incremental steps that move you closer to your goal can have a remarkable effect on your life, even if you don't notice them yourself. You spend every day with yourself, so the gradual changes that occur daily can easily go unnoticed by you, yet may be seen by others. It is similar to a frog, which will jump out of boiling water as it recognizes the drastic change and knows it is too hot. However, if you put a frog in room temperature water and gradually heat it, the frog will not jump out, the incremental increases in temperature go unnoticed. Do you feel like you're making deliberate decisions to move toward your goals? Or do you feel you're standing still unaware of what is happening?

Are you willing to put that extra cash aside for your future now? It could mean a lot.

When it comes to money it seems many people do not notice the gradual changes and the impact these small things can have. You may feel that if you cannot save thousands a month, why save at all? Have you ever felt that way?

What could $100 a month do? This thinking reminds me of an example where people are asked if they would prefer to get $1 million in 30 days, or a penny today doubling for 30 days (two cents the second day, four cents the third day, and so on). Which would you choose? You might be quick to say the $1 million, but let's take a look. If you decided to take the penny route, after a week you would have 64 cents and might be questioning your choice. It has been a week and it doesn't seem much is happening as you do not even have a dollar. After two weeks pass, you check the account and you only have $81.92—ouch. It has been two weeks and nothing major has happened, so what could happen over the same time frame going forward? You let another week pass before checking your account, and it is Day 21 of the 30 and you currently have $10,485.76.

That's it? By now it may seem all that time has passed and since nothing exceptional has happened, you may want to stop and take no further action. You have stuck to your promise, done the right thing, made the small gradual changes and felt no big payoff. Have you ever given up on a goal because you felt it was still too far away? If you continue to strive through, push forward, and continue to stay the course, you may be closer to the goal than you noticed. So how long does it take for the patience of the gradual penny growth for you to have more than a million dollars? On Day 28, you would cross the threshold to see $1,342,177.28 in your account and you still have two more days. On day 30 you would have over $5 million in your account, a much greater amount than you could have taken originally and substantially more than if you would have stopped after 3 weeks. See, small changes can equate to big differences if you stick with them, have patience, and trust that your path will work out. Are you willing to put that extra cash aside for your future now? It could mean a lot.

CHAPTER 6

The Benefits of Working with a Professional

It is not the knowing that is difficult, but the doing.

- African Proverb

NOW LET'S LOOK at how best to pull everything together and put a plan in place to help you create a path to your goals. Remember that nobody makes it alone in this world. Even the best and brightest rely on others to guide them and facilitate new saving or investing opportunities.

If you're serious about achieving your goals in the most effective and efficient way—or about making sure that you're on the right track, consider using a professional financial advisor. A professional can help bring your goals into sharper focus or suggest new ways to get there. When it comes to your short-term goals, whether a month or a year out, you should be able to make small tweaks here and there to help you get there. Whether that means using the 30-day challenge to find new ways to save money or opening that savings account so you can start putting money aside. With some action you will begin to build momentum going toward your goal. It could be as simple as taking a goal and working backwards to today, to find out how much you need to save.

For example, let's say you have a short-term goal of saving an extra $1,000 over the next two months. You know that you have roughly 60 days to get to that goal. You know that small steps today can make a difference, so you do the math and figure out that if you save about $16.67 a day, at the end of 60 days, you will reach your goal.

An advisor can answer questions, figure out how to start, and help you create a plan.

With your long-term goals, that may be a little more difficult. You may not even see the path or know where to start. In these situations, it is a good idea to get professional assistance. An advisor can answer questions, figure out how to start, and help you create a plan.

When I'm working with clients on drafting a roadmap for them, there are many assumptions and details that get clarified. I work with clients to understand their goals and we take the time to find out the details, such as where they want to live, how they see themselves living in retirement, how much money they will need to support that lifestyle and the family, people, and organizations that are important to them.

Additionally, you want to make sure that any investment choices reflect the "why" of your goal and fit within the risks you are willing to take. It is important to address your "why" because it can change the investment selection today. For example, let's say that in five years you wanted to make a large purchase, such as paying cash for a new car. Since you will need that entire amount of money available, you would want an investment that provides you access to that lump sum. On the other hand, if in five years you wanted to start withdrawing money slowly to supplement your income or for retirement, you would need cash flow, rather than a lump sum. Even though both examples are for the same time frame and have the same starting amount, the investment choice would be different.

Additionally, if you are a very risk-averse person who would lose sleep if the markets dropped and caused your accounts to go down, you will want to make sure that the plan doesn't have you in investments that would cause you anxiety and lower your present-day enjoyment. There is a fine balance in the planning process and with the time you have spent thinking about your goals—your "why"—it will be much easier to strike that balance and confidently move forward.

Combat Common Fears

I come across a lot of people who feel that they either haven't saved enough money or don't know where to start creating financial goals, so they don't do anything. They freeze, overwhelmed by all of the information thrown at them, and have no idea if they have a foundation for their financial future. If that is you, relax. Decide right now that your future is worth a few minutes today spent thinking about the concepts in this book. Make a plan and start to execute.

If you are late to saving and planning for your future, it is going to be all right. You simply need to start moving forward. At these later stages, it is important that you don't make dramatic mistakes, but rather learn from other people's mistakes, as you do not have time to rebuild again. It is important to have experience and expertise on your side, guiding you through the waters. Why is it so important? As we get closer to our goals, especially the financial goal of retirement, losses in a portfolio can have long-lasting impacts. When you are younger, you can wait it out, continue to save more money and invest properly to have that money recuperated. But as you get older, the time is more important and you have less room to wait things out.

Who knows how long it will take for you to see returns of that magnitude and get back to where you started? That is why working with a professional and understanding your goals is so important.

Let's look at an example of a market correction on a portfolio, and determine how much of a return would be required to get back to even. I have found that many people think that if the stock market goes down by 10 percent, that they need a 10 percent return to get back to where they started. Unfortunately, that is not the case. If the stock market goes down by 10 percent, you will actually need 11 percent to get back to even. That may not seem like a big difference, but it is a minor loss. Let's say that your portfolio experiences a 20 percent loss, how much do you need to return to get back to where you started? Your portfolio would have to gain 25 percent or a quarter of its overall value, just to get you back to even. Think of it like this: If you have $10 and you lost 20 percent, you'd have $8. With that amount, you would need $2 or 25 percent to get back to where you started. Who knows how long it will take for you to see returns of that magnitude and get back to where you started? That is why working with a professional and understanding your goals is so important.

You want to create a portfolio that gets you to your goal with the least amount of risk possible. If, based on your assumptions, you need an expected return of seven percent to achieve your goal, it would be prudent to create a portfolio that generates that return with minimal risk.

Another benefit of this strategy is that while the stock market goes through its up and down swings, you won't make reactive, emotional decisions based on its moves. Rather, you will focus on the things you can control, look at your specific investments, and know what your target is and how that equates to your goals. The markets will continue to move, the next hot stock tip will still be talked about, but you can take comfort in knowing that your portfolio is solid enough to withstand shocks.

Risky Business

Let's touch on risk and diversification for a second, as the risk in your investments will affect how you feel about them. When things are looking good and performing well, it is easy to stay invested and take on more risk. It is in the tough times, when the markets are going down, that making proper investment decisions is difficult. It's hard to save money when you feel you're losing money, or to stay invested when you emotionally want to start selling.

Diversification can help in these instances, although just buying more investments doesn't necessarily mean you have proper diversification. If everything in your portfolio is moving in the same direction, you may not have true diversification. There will usually be something in your portfolio that is doing poorly when the rest is performing well.

I know it is difficult to look at the one part of your portfolio that's down when everything else is up, but consider the opposite: What if everything else was down and now that one thing is performing well? What diversification does is allow the volatility or swings in the portfolio to be reduced.

Again, this gets you to your expected return needs in the smoothest way possible. What I help my clients understand is their plan and the return they need for their plan. Then we look for ways to generate that return in the smoothest way possible. Why take on the unnecessary additional risk?

Naturally Excel

Up to this point I have discussed the different steps toward creating your goals. You looked at your goals and asked yourself why you wanted them so you could find the core qualities you desire for your future.

Now, I'd like to switch gears and discuss your strengths in order to see what you thrive at—where you feel at ease and can naturally accomplish great things.

You may be asking yourself, what does this have to do with financial planning? Well, your financial future has to do with you and your goals, so it's important to understand them well. It's also important to remember that if you're working with an advisor, make sure it's someone who has taken the time to understand you and your strengths and weaknesses.

A trusted, knowledgeable advisor who understands you can put together a plan that highlights your strengths and areas you naturally excel at, making it more likely you will accomplish your goals.

You may feel that your goals are just out of your grasp when you spend too much time focusing on what you're not doing right or how far behind you are. Instead, I'd rather you focus on the things you have done right. As you focus your attention on those actions, you will do more of the right things and use those strengths and talents to help you reach your goals.

Think about the talents that you tend to gravitate toward. As you recall these activities, do you start to recognize a theme or areas where you excel?

When I asked a client, Brittney, these questions, she paused and looked at me for a moment. She then said she was in the process of starting her own consulting firm because she recognized her passion was helping to connect people and grow businesses. She explained how she would sit down with startup business executives for hours, learning about their needs and wants for their own enterprises and then help create strategies to get their businesses moving. She would get lost in the creative process for hours, trying to connect the dots, drafting ideas, and looking for opportunities. It was that ability to stay energized and excited in her work that inspired her to start her own firm and assured her it was the correct career.

Exercise 14: The Thrive List

Hopefully, like Brittney, your career is one of your strengths and truly brings you joy. But it's probably not the only place you excel. I would like you to look at all areas of your life and the strengths you have in each area. You may be engaged in activities that may not be the greatest use of your time, or even worse, that drain you of your energy. Making yourself do things that drain your energy, patience, creativity, and desire does not do you any good. It would be better to focus on the areas where you thrive and accomplish more along the way. Make a list of the things that you are truly good at and that bring you joy as you do them, whether it's connecting with people, researching new ideas, creative work, or anything else.

I was working with a married couple, the Jacobs, on creating an investment portfolio for them. The husband, John, had always taken care of their investments himself, wanting that control. However, Julie thought they could be doing better and that was the reason for our meeting. She knew John had the best of intentions, but investing was not an area in which he thrived. She would watch him on weekends, struggling for hours reading and researching investments and the latest news, trying to figure out the market, all the while becoming more frustrated and withdrawn.

Julie wanted him to be spending time with her, enjoying their life and the things that brought them happiness, not sitting at a desk frustrated. They both spent long hours at the office during the week, had good careers, and excelled in their fields while staying diligent about saving. At the beginning of the meeting John was a little hesitant, but as we talked he loosened up a bit.

On the topic of his work, the excitement started to bubble through and continued to build as he mentioned future projects. As the conversation progressed, we got to their goals and why he felt the need to manage their investments himself. He noted how he felt that all advisors offered the same things and so he couldn't find a benefit to using one. John was great at articulating his goals and how he envisioned their future. He had spent the time to really craft meaningful "whys." It was in the implementation that he fluttered. So, John was able to communicate what they were working toward and together we crafted a plan to help them get there. Now he's enjoying his weekends by spending time with his family, while Julie revels in their time together doing what makes them happy.

A Personal Approach

There is a lot of information available about financial advice, advisors and firms. I know at times it can seem overwhelming, and as John had noticed, it can seem that they all offer the same thing. To add some clarity and simplify the process, let's look at key factors along with your goals.

Your goals deserve more than that. Life doesn't fit nicely in five pie charts.

One of the reasons you want to work with a professional advisor you trust is to help you create a path toward your goals and put forth a strategic plan to lay out steps to help you. The plan you create should be similar to your goals in that it is specific and measurable.

Remember the MAPS strategy for drafting goals (Measurable, Actionable, Personal and Specific). Your plan should have all of these attributes as well. The plan should be customized to your personal goals, your risk tolerance and time frame, with the steps easily identifiable. You want to make sure that you are not bundled into a firm's generic, pre-packaged, pie-chart-heavy solution.

I have had many conversations with friends and clients regarding their feelings of being put into a pie-chart solution that they have seen at their bank. They don't like it. After all the time they spent talking to their representative, it all came tumbling down to being shown five pie charts, varying by risk. You may wonder, "How is that it?" Your goals deserve more than that. Life doesn't fit nicely in five pie charts.

This is why I take the time to learn about my clients, hear their specific goals and find their "why" before creating a custom portfolio. By using a broad investment universe, more than just traditional stocks and bonds that you would expect to see, I am able to customize the portfolio and provide access to more opportunities for my clients to prosper. The capabilities I offer include real estate, private equity, lending, development, futures, commodities, and the options go on and on. With that, you will be able to have investments that are well diversified, customized to your needs and have the potential to profit in different market conditions, which will help you meet your goals. An added benefit is that it is done within the risk profile that you feel comfortable with.

CHAPTER 7

How to Pick the Right Professional

The road to success is lined with
many tempting parking spaces.

- Traditional Proverb

CONGRATULATIONS! NOW YOU'VE defined
your goals, wants, desires and really gotten to the
center of your "why."

When looking for different ways to get your money
working for you, it is a good idea to have a trusted
professional to help you create a financial road map,
to hold you accountable to your goals, and to oversee
everything. Toward that end, you may decide to
work with a financial advisor.

Looking for a financial advisor can be tough, and not
knowing the ins and outs of the industry, you may
feel at a disadvantage. With a quick internet search
of financial advisors, it is easy to see the disparity in
the title. From your neighborhood insurance agent to
a random real estate agent trying to position
themselves differently, the vast amount of so-called

financial advisors can be overwhelming. Add to it the do-it-yourself programs and other automatic investment brokers and most people don't know how to proceed and wind up doing nothing. You are different though. At this point, you know your goals and your desires, and you have a passion to make them a reality. So, you'll take the time to do some research and take action.

> *That is why it is so important to work with an advisor who will help you define your goals and understand your true "why"—or for you to have your goals defined before looking for an advisor.*

What Makes a Good Advisor?

An advisor can help you in taking action to achieve your goals by helping you leverage your resources and time. There is a vast universe of resources available to you from people, products, and books to assist you in achieving the goals you have outlined.

The question now is how to access those people and the most efficient way for you to move forward. With that, it is worthwhile to use a financial advisor to help you structure the plan, find products, and hold you accountable along your path.

When looking to find an advisor, it's important to keep your goals in mind. Each firm, person or group may have a different solution to getting to your goals. That is why it is so important to work with an advisor who will help you define your goals and understand your true "why"—or for you to have your goals defined before looking for an advisor. You want to make sure that the advisor's capabilities match or are in line with your goals. In addition, you want to make sure that you have room for honest communication.

There are many ways to find advisors—you can ask your friends and family to help you compile a list. I find it best to ask your other advisors, whether they be your CPA, attorney, banker or coach, for a few referrals. From that list, there are numerous resources where you can check the background and licensing of the advisors, such as on the websites of the Securities and Exchange Commission and the Financial Industry Regulatory Authority. This will give you a better understanding of the capabilities of the advisor, as it will tell you the licenses that they hold.

Again, it is important that these capabilities match what you're looking to achieve. Each state maintains an insurance division, which will show you the licensing of that person related to insurance, so you will want to check with your state insurance division to find out if they are licensed.

To add another layer, each firm has different options that they allow their representatives to offer clients. So, it is a good practice to include varying institutions, from large banks to independent groups and small teams.

Now that we know that not all advisors are the same, you know the benefit of looking into the background and capabilities of the firm. You see, saying you are a financial advisor is like saying you're a doctor. When I say I'm a doctor, you may have a different thought, but most likely it's positive and comes with some type of power or prestige. However, if you met a stranger on the street and they said only their title, doctor, would you trust them to cut open your leg and stitch you up? What about something less intrusive—would you take medication that they handed you out of their pocket? Of course not! You have no idea their background, their specialty or even that they are actually a physician. For all you know they could be a Ph.D. in mathematics toting around the doctor title. You're clearly in need of more context before moving forward. You need to do the same thing with a financial advisor. That way, once you see everyone's proposals, you can pick the one that you are most comfortable with and that will help you to your goals, as there are many different investment options to help you.

If you are working with an advisor whose menu doesn't fit you, you may want to look around for a better option based on what you are looking for.

I had a friend come up to me one day and ask if I was a fee-only fiduciary advisor. Puzzled, I asked him why he was asking. He mentioned that he had been talking with a fee-only advisor who had told him that it was the only way to go because fiduciary advisors have to put their clients' interest first.

Now, I have the capacity to work as a fiduciary and much more, but I thought my friend was missing a valuable piece of information. See, what is best for each person will vary based on the advisor they choose to work with and that person's capabilities.

Just because someone tells you they have the best option for you, remember, that it is based on what they have to offer. For example, let's say you and a friend were making dinner plans and she decided to pick the restaurant. She is excited that you are going to her new favorite restaurant. When you arrive at the restaurant, you discover it is a steakhouse, which would be fine except you just gave up meat and are only eating seafood. You know she is excited so you don't say anything and join her. As you look at the menu you realize they have one seafood option, so you decide to order it since it is the only thing you can eat.

That was the best option for you at that particular restaurant. On the other hand, if she had picked a seafood restaurant, your options would have been much different. You would have had an entire menu of dishes you could eat. If you felt like fish, lobster, crab, or scallops, they would have been available for you. Now to think that the steakhouse was your best option would not be fitting based on knowing the menu at the seafood restaurant.

In the financial industry it's the same thing. An advisor could take you to a steakhouse or a seafood restaurant. You want to be clear before you do business with him or her. If you are working with an advisor whose menu doesn't fit you, you may want to look around for a better option based on your goals.

Make a Decision

Once you've narrowed down the list to a few candidates, it is always good to have a conversation with each team. You want to make sure that their values, communication style and demeanor match with what you were looking for. It is extremely important that you have open, meaningful communication with the advisor as well. This is your life, your finances, your future. You will be sharing very intimate details of your financial future, your goals and wants with this person, so you must know that you can openly share with them and that they listen and account for your desires.

It is also important that the advisor you select is open to having communication with the rest of your team, such as your CPA, attorney or anybody else that you feel is important to your goals. This communication amongst your team is invaluable. It will ensure that there are seamless transitions, everyone is on the same page and that everything flows as it should in the most efficient way possible. You want to make sure your team is working in the same direction and building your future together.

You will notice nowhere so far have I mentioned fees, performance or any of the other questions that seem to be at the forefront of many campaigns. There is a lot of marketing on low costs, lowest fees, and other things. And while these are important, they are secondary to your goal.

The most important part of your advisor relationship is the open communication and access to investments and solutions that most efficiently achieve your goals. When it comes to other aspects of our lives we do not always pick the cheapest product just because it is less expensive.

So why, when it comes to your financial future, would you make a decision because it's cheap? Many of us eat organic, which can be more expensive than eating traditionally. We probably don't drive the base model of our car because it was cheaper than the model with all of the goodies. If you are not skimping in your transportation, why would you skimp in your future? We all know you get what you pay for, and your goals are too important to go cheap.

Most advisors charge in a similar range, and you will be able to see the difference on the proposals. But if you have your goal and the advisor put together a plan that gets you to that goal, in a manner you like, does a reasonable cost matter? You want to achieve your goal and now have a plan to do so.

We have all been so inundated with advertising that drives down to these small factors that we've lost sight of the true goal, the true purpose of the financial advisor: to help clients define their goals and create a plan to get there. Each plan is unique and each advisor's investment within the plan is different, so focus on your goals and do not mind the smaller stuff. It isn't going to get you any closer to your goals, to the life you want for yourself. The small stuff will simply drain you of your passion, purpose and clarity and leave you feeling tired and confused.

Additionally, an advisor may have an advantage to a particular goal or offer a solution to a problem you have. If the least expensive answer can't help you reach your goals, it doesn't matter that it's cheap; it doesn't apply to you. Again, the most important thing when looking at this is how it affects your ability to achieve your goals in the most efficient way possible.

Know What You're Buying

When I'm meeting with individuals about their investment portfolios, I spend a lot of time educating them on ideas, theories, and general investing. The investments we use are far enough outside of the everyday conversation that it takes time for the concepts to sink in. It is possible to invest in more than publicly traded stocks and bonds, and there are opportunities to invest in themes or ideas and find ways to capitalize on them. It could be as simple as something you use every day and being able to generate a return from an investment in that theme.

Here's what I mean: take an example of depositing money into a savings account at a bank versus taking a personal loan from the bank, as we know that banks take in deposits and then lend those funds out to customers. If you walked into a bank today and made a deposit, the interest rate you would receive from the bank would be low, in the neighborhood of one percent. So, your money is generating a one percent return for you. Now, if you walked into that same bank for a personal loan, they would likely charge you eight percent or higher, depending on your credit.

The important thing to realize here is that the bank keeps the spread between what it gives on deposits and what it charges on loans. In this example, you can get a one percent return or be charged eight percent. I don't know about you, but instead of those options, I would rather be earning that eight percent. That could have a significant impact on my investment returns and my ability to reach my goals. So, we can think like a bank, find ways to invest in lending opportunities and generate returns.

It is this change in perspective and willingness to think outside the box that can help you get there. Now you might be thinking that eight percent doesn't sound like a lot. A lot of people come to me with ideas of the returns they want. For some reason, it seems that ten percent is the number they like to use. When I start asking them about where that number came from, it is usually equity returns and no mention of the risks, or "a friend that has been doing this for years." I'm sure you have heard the saying, "If it's too good to be true, it probably is," and it is a saying for good reason. Nothing is perfect, and everything will have drawbacks. It is important to learn all that you can, do your due diligence and ask questions.

Before you make a purchase uncover the areas where something is not perfect, where the risks are, and be comfortable with them or do not move forward. I always want my clients to know both sides of the story, to have all the facts, as it helps build trust and understanding when both sides of the communication are honest.

CHAPTER 8

Live Your Life

Today well lived makes every yesterday a dream of
happiness, and every tomorrow a vision of hope.
Look well, therefore, to this day.

- Indian Proverb

WITH YOUR PLAN in hand and your advisor by
your side, you are equipped with the resources to
assist you along your financial journey. As the years
go by, you will be able to consciously look at your
plan and see if you are on course or drifting away
from your goals.

When you know that you are drifting, you can adjust
the course and make those minor corrections to get
back on track. If you fail to notice that you are
drifting off course, your advisor will hold you
accountable and make sure you are aware.

Along with that, with open communication and
annual updates, you will be aware of the progress
you are making, be reminded of your goals, and
make appropriate changes. You won't wake up ten
years from now, where you want to be by accident.
You don't just appear there. You get there by the
choices you make today and over the course of those
ten years.

That is why it is so important to have the plan and an advisor to assist you and make sure you are paying attention to your goals, your finances, and making adjustments when necessary. By doing these minor adjustments, you will make certain you are moving in the direction of your goals along the way.

> *When you know where you are and have a goal of where you want to go, there is one more important thing to remember: you need to enjoy today.*

When you know where you are and have a goal of where you want to go, there is one more important thing to remember: you need to enjoy today. It is important to be present in the moment while being inspired by your goals. When you have the ability to do both, you will notice more opportunities to get to your goals and you will be happier today.

You will feel that you have a purpose and will start to develop a deep enthusiasm for today. With that enthusiasm, it is easier, almost automatic, to move in the direction of your goals. You can brush aside any obstacle that may come up and find ways to circumvent the challenge instead of fighting it.

The momentum you will create is a powerful force that will snowball and continue to help build your enthusiasm each day while instilling further confidence in yourself and your abilities.

You will start to notice more opportunities arise to help you move forward. You will have the courage and energy to take those opportunities and pursue them.

Enjoy the Journey

A lot of people may feel that until they reach the destination or have all the material things they desire, they can't be happy. That doesn't resonate for me, as I want to be happy today. Don't you? The idea that I should wait for something to occur before I can be happy doesn't sit well. I know that I can enjoy today, live for today, and it will be a good day. That isn't to say there are no bad days—they still happen—there are days you feel off, days you don't want to get out of bed. Days like this happen to everyone. Rather than be dragged down by them, shake it off, do what you need to do and move back toward happiness.

This reminds me of the differences in how traffic seems depending on where you're going. There is always traffic in Southern California, and when you are trapped in it, trying to get to work or home, it can be dreadful. It can stress you out and exhaust you.

Now, when I have a weekend getaway planned and my friends and I are driving out of town, if we hit traffic, it doesn't faze us. We are listening to music, laughing, and talking about the weekend ahead with complete disregard for the traffic. We may be the envy of other cars on the road as we are having fun, even while sitting in traffic. My friends and I know where we are going and what is in store, so we can enjoy the journey getting there much more. It doesn't matter if we are a few hours late to our destination, there is nothing we can do about that. So, we embrace the moment, make the best of it, and laugh.

In the introduction I mentioned how, over the course of a year, I had gone from never having sailed, to learning how to sail. I had the goal of getting one certification and seeing where that led. I knew that I would enjoy being on the water and that the challenge of powering a boat with only wind would be enticing. Once I got started, it was an amazing experience to be cruising down the coast, enjoying the peace and tranquility that accompanied the sounds of the water flowing along the hull. I created my goal, even though I did not know the exact journey I was going to take.

A lot of times, people feel the same way—you know what you want, but you don't know all the steps, so you don't do anything. I prefer a different method. I prefer to know where I am and where I want to go, and then go. I like to start taking actions toward my desired outcome and see where the journey leads. As you take action and build momentum, things start to move a little easier. If your course needs to be changed, it is a simple shift to course correct.

The important thing is not to try to control every aspect, but rather to keep moving. In my case, the goal of one certification has grown to much more than I could have expected. I went with the flow and earned six certifications, competed in the Newport to Ensenada International Yacht Race and have made great friends along the way. I would have never been able to experience all of that had I tried to plan every step of the journey before I started. I wouldn't have been able to imagine all of the different adventures I have had. The opportunities and experiences still continue to build.

During the journey, my "why" changed as well. I went from a desire to do one specific thing, earn a sailing certificate, to a "why" much bigger than myself, as I watch how my family and friends have come together, the joy it brings to them, and how sharing my new passion has spread happiness.

Creating your financial future is similar in that you do not need to know every step or have everything figured out in order to get there. Simply know where you'd like to go and start taking action to move in that direction.

As you get more comfortable with the uncertainty of not knowing every financial move, you will slowly build momentum toward achieving your goal and the right course will emerge.

What does the culmination of all your hard work, passion and effort look like? That is easy. It is whatever you want.

What does the culmination of all your hard work, passion and effort look like? That is easy. It is whatever you want. It is you realizing your stated goals. It is you spending the time to learn your values and priorities, to harness your "why," and to take action. When that moment of success occurs, it is a great experience and makes all of the time and energy worth it. It is in these moments where it all magically happens.

Get There!

When people ask me why I am an advisor or what the best part of my job is, it is hands down this moment of success. To support my clients and watch them grow from not knowing their "why" and owning a random investment portfolio, to a clear, concise "why" that they can articulate, and a strategic investment portfolio with a plan to guide them to the future they desire. To watch their journeys unfold along the way, to hear their stories and see their successes, is an amazing experience.

I remember one of the most touching moments in my career. I was sitting with my client, Tom, in his office and he was stressed out. Tom had called me two days prior in a panic as his wife, Marilyn, wanted to retire and he didn't feel that he could afford it. See, Tom had always had a vision to retire when Marilyn was ready and spend more time living their passion of playing golf at different courses around the world. He loved his wife immensely and wanted to be able to do that with her. Tom had recently had a few setbacks in business and had to cover some unforeseen expenses, meaning money had flown out of the accounts. He felt there was no way his investments could have held up.

He had stuck his head in the sand when it came to the investments as he knew I was watching over them. So, with Marilyn discussing retirement, he had called me to schedule a meeting. He knew it was time to look at the effects of the last few years and see where he stood. I told him I would run some scenarios and illustrations on how much he could expect to withdraw from his accounts. When I walked into his office that morning, he sat slouched in his chair with a defeated look in his eyes. As he finished sharing the conversation he had with Marilyn, he slouched further in the chair and asked me, "How much damage have my accounts taken? Am I going to have to work until I'm 90?" Have you ever felt that way?

I pulled out the illustration, put it on the desk and sat next to Tom. Before he could even look at the documents, he looked at me and shared that he hadn't looked at a statement in over a year. Although we had conversations to discuss the portfolio and allocation changes, he had no idea how much was left in the accounts. As we flipped through the illustration, we finally arrived to the critical page, the withdraw rate and the corresponding dollar amount he could expect to receive. Tom looked down at the number and without saying anything, looked up at me with a puzzled gaze and slowly looked back down at the number. We sat in silence for over a minute as Tom gathered his thoughts. He finally pulled his eyes from the page and asked, "Is that per year?" I replied, "No, that would be the monthly amount you will receive."

Tom immediately broke out in tears, overcome with joy and happiness, as it seemed the weight of the world had been lifted from his shoulders. He hugged me as the happiness continued to overcome him and thanked me for looking after him and his family. I couldn't help but get teary-eyed myself.

It is in the moments such as Tom's, that I feel the fulfillment of my passion and want to help more people define their why and create the financial paths to get there. To see the moment when your dreams come true after your long journey. My greatest hope is that you have the experience of achieving your desires. That you take the information you've learned in this book, define your passion, find the support and guidance you need and create the life of your desires.

And, of course, remember to enjoy the journey, it can lead to even greater moments, once you finally...

Get There!

About the Author

Ken Kladouris, MBA

When you think of the life you want to live, what will bring you joy, happiness, and fulfillment? This question started Ken Kladouris on the path to living a more meaningful life. After clarifying his "why" he literally threw caution to the wind before exceeding even his own expectations!

After years of working as a wealth manager, the soon-to-be sea farer knew there was more to life than earning degrees, making more money, and receiving accolades. While achieving all these career moves on land, he listened to his calling and was drawn to the lessons he would learn at sea. Just as the massive blue ocean continuously gives back to its own, he desired to give back too—something most money managers don't have top of mind.

His personal search for meaning and fulfillment have led him on a quest to help others go beyond a sound financial plan. Ken's accolades are many. Ken earned his Bachelor's degree in Business Administration from California State University, Long Beach, and his MBA with a concentration in Finance from Pepperdine University, in Malibu, CA. He holds the Financial Industry Regulatory Authority (FINRA) Series 3, 7, 24, 31 and 66 registrations as well as a California Life & Health Insurance license. But those aren't what sets Ken apart from other financial experts.

As your guide, Ken will help you move forward and create a stronger, more balanced future so that you can live the life you want to live by removing the confusion and overwhelming emotions around financial planning. Ken will help you align your life's purpose with your financial future to help you Get There.

Ken is also the author of *Get There! Chart Your Course to Financial Abundance and Live the Life You Desire.* This book guides readers to create a vision, mission, and plan for their life.

When Ken is not helping clients create purpose-filled life plans, he enjoys being an active member in the community and spending time with his family, preferable on the on the water, whether sailing or aboard a powerboat.

Quotes from the Book

Go confidently in the direction of your dreams. Live the life you have imagined. - Henry David Thoreau

Don't set sail on someone else's star. - African Proverb

The best time to plant a tree was 20 years ago. The second-best time is now. - Chinese Proverb

For tomorrow belongs to the people who prepare for it today. - African Proverb

A journey of a thousand miles begins with a single step.   - Chinese Proverb

It is not the knowing that is difficult, but the doing.
- African Proverb

The road to success is lined with many tempting parking spaces.   - Traditional Proverb

Today well lived makes every yesterday a dream of happiness, and every tomorrow a vision of hope. Look well, therefore, to this day.   - Indian Proverb

Contact Ken

Ken Kladouris

For all speaking and media inquiries, please visit:

www.KenKladouris.com

Made in the USA
San Bernardino, CA
06 January 2019